The KidHaven Science Library

Plate Tectonics

by Linda George

KIDHAVEN PRESS™

THOMSON
™
GALE

San Diego • Detroit • New York • San Francisco • Cleveland
New Haven, Conn. • Waterville, Maine • London • Munich

THOMSON

GALE™

On cover: The San Andreas Fault, one hundred miles north of Los Angeles, California.

Cover photo: © G. Gerster/Photo Researchers
© Jonathan Blair/CORBIS, 21
© Christie's Images/CORBIS, 23
© Corel Corporation, 15, 16
DigitalStock, 18
© David Hardy/Science Photo Library/Photo Researchers, 5
© Dr. Ken MacDonald/Science Photo Library/Photo Researchers, 9
© NASA/SPL/Photo Researchers, Inc./25
National Oceanic and Atmospheric Association, 27, 31, 37
Brandy Noon, 6, 7, 11, 19, 24, 33
© Roger Ressmeyer/CORBIS, 38, 40
© Paul A. Souders/CORBIS, 12
© David Weintraub/Photo Researchers, 28
© Michael S. Yamashita/CORBIS, 35

© 2003 by KidHaven Press. KidHaven Press is an imprint of The Gale Group, Inc., a division of Thomson Learning, Inc.

KidHaven™ and Thomson Learning™ are trademarks used herein under license.

For more information, contact
KidHaven Press
27500 Drake Rd.
Farmington Hills, MI 48331-3535
Or you can visit our Internet site at http://www.gale.com

LIBRARY OF CONGRESS CATALOGING-IN-PUBLICATION DATA

George, Linda.
    Plate tectonics / by Linda George.
      v. cm. — (The kidhaven science library)
Includes bibliographical references and index.
Summary: Discusses how continents move, how mountains are formed, volcanoes, and what occurs during an earthquake.
    ISBN 0-7377-1405-0 (hbk. : alk. paper)
1. Plate tectonics—Juvenile literature. [1. Plate tectonics. 2. Volcanoes.
3. Earthquakes.] I. Title. II. Series.
    QE511.4 .G47 2003
    551.1'36—dc21

                                                2002006245

Printed in the United States of America

Contents

Chapter 1
How Continents Move. 4

Chapter 2
How Mountains Form 14

Chapter 3
Mountains of Fire 22

Chapter 4
When the Earth Shakes 32

Glossary 42

For Further Exploration 44

Index 47

How Continents Move

When planet Earth formed billions of years ago, it was extremely hot and made of molten, or melted, rock. As the planet cooled, a **crust** formed on the surface, much like a crust forms on chocolate pudding when it cools. Eventually, the crust broke apart into pieces, called **plates**. These plates are about thirty to fifty miles thick. The plates float on the hot interior of the earth—much like crackers on a bowl of hot soup.

Heat from deep inside the earth causes the plates to move. Earth's continents sit on these plates. So, when the plates move, the continents move with them. This movement is very slow. On average, the plates move about as fast as fingernails grow—an inch or so each year. The movement of these plates is called **plate tectonics**.

There are two types of tectonic plates. Continental plates are found primarily under continents, and oceanic plates are found primarily

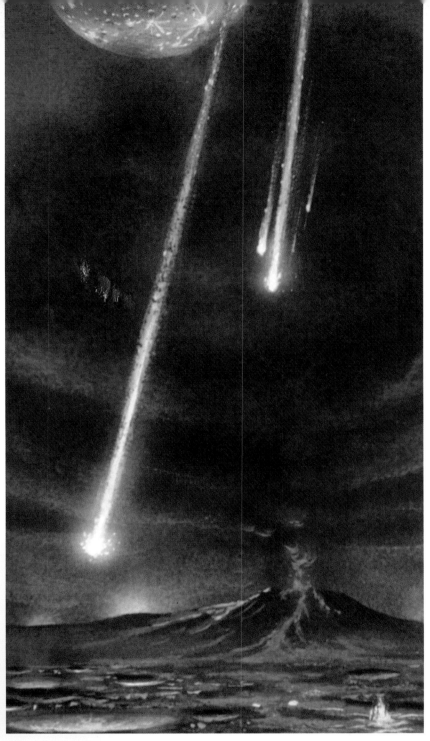

An illustration shows how Earth may have looked billions of years ago as it developed from molten rock.

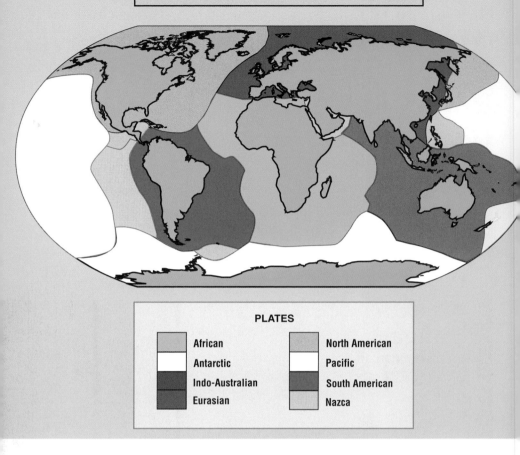

Earth's Tectonic Plates

PLATES

African

Antarctic

Indo-Australian

Eurasian

North American

Pacific

South American

Nazca

under oceans. The largest plates include the North American, South American, Pacific, Indo-Australian, Nazca, Eurasian, African, and Antarctic plates. The smaller plates include the Juan de Fuca, Arabian, Cocos, Philippine, Caribbean, and Scotia plates.

The plates move constantly, and when they move different things happen. Sometimes they collide or move apart. Other times they slide side by side, going in the same or in different directions. These different movements bring about incredible changes on the surface of the earth. It was not until the early years of the twentieth century that scientists had an explanation for this process.

How Were the Plates Discovered?

In 1910, while looking at a map, a German scientist noticed something interesting about the shape of Earth's continents. When placed side by side, they seemed to fit together like giant puzzle pieces. The scientist, Alfred Lothan Wegener,

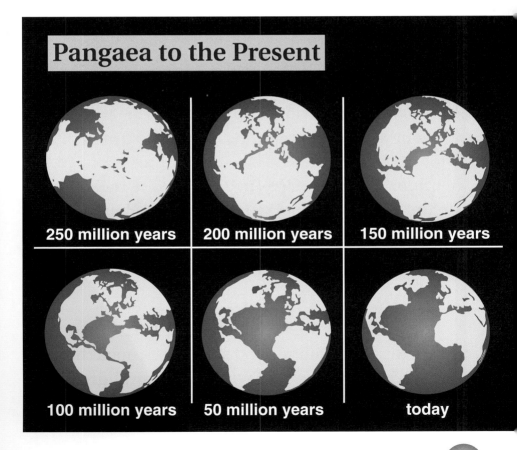

Pangaea to the Present

250 million years   200 million years   150 million years

100 million years   50 million years   today

realized that the pieces formed what looked like one big continent. Mountain ranges seemed to line up when he put the maps of the continents together. Wegener also knew that certain types of rock and certain plant and animal fossils had been found on more than one continent. All of this suggested to Wegener that, long ago, the continents might have been part of one large continent. He called this supercontinent **Pangaea**, a word that means "all land."

Wegener's theory explained how this huge continent gradually broke into pieces. The pieces formed smaller continents that drifted until they reached the positions they hold today. He guessed that this splitting and movement of continents took about 200 million years.

Other scientists did not believe Wegener's theory. It seemed impossible that such huge pieces of land could drift from one place to another. Wegener died in 1930 unable to prove his controversial theory. Years later, though, scientists learned something that gave new weight to Wegener's ideas.

Mapping the Ocean Floors

Until the 1940s, scientists believed that ocean floors were made of the oldest rock on the planet. They also believed that the weight of the ocean's waters had pressed the floor flat. New technology allowed scientists to test these ideas.

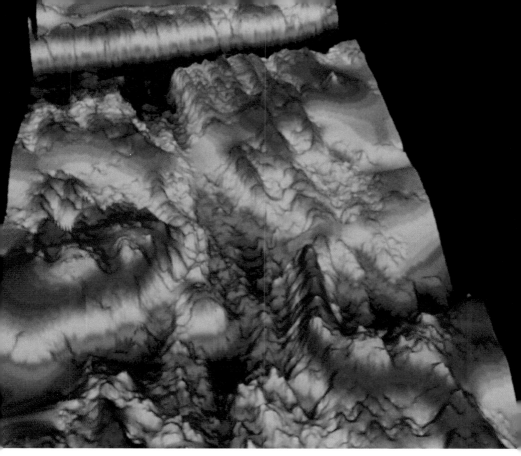

This sonar map of the ocean floor shows the Mid-Atlantic Ridge (vertical blue stripe). The horizontal blue stripes are other deep faults and valleys.

Using radar and sonar, they were able to bounce sound waves off the ocean floor. They expected to find a largely flat floor covered with many feet of silt and mud. To their surprise, they found mountains and valleys, much taller and deeper than any on dry land.

Down the middle of the Atlantic Ocean was a huge range of undersea mountains that extended 47,000 miles from Iceland to Antarctica. This ridge towered 6,000 to 10,000 feet above the ocean floor. Surveyors called these mountains the Mid-Atlantic Ridge. Down the middle of the ridge was a deep valley. After scooping rock from the ocean floor and figuring out how old it was, surveyors discovered that the rock around the ridge was much younger than expected. Instead of being billions of years old, like Earth itself, the rock around the ridge was only 150 million years old. But, that did not seem possible.

The only explanation was that the valley down the middle of the ridge had formed when the mountain range split in two. This caused a crack in the earth's crust, down the middle of the ridge. Molten rock from deep inside the earth bubbled up through the crack. Then, it cooled and hardened in the cold ocean waters, forming new rock. This meant the seafloor was spreading. The rock of the ocean floors rested on huge plates that were moving away from each other. Wegener had guessed right, and now scientists had proof of his theory, called **continental drift**.

Fossil Remains Prove Continental Drift

Further proof was gained by comparing fossil remains of plants and animals on different continents. Remains of a reptile called Mesosaurus have been found in Africa and in South America. These two continents are about 3,200 miles apart. Fossil remains of another reptile, Lystrosaurus, have been found in Africa and in Antarctica, which are about 2,400 miles apart. Stegosaurus fossils have been found in Texas and in India. Fossils of the insect Diadectid have been found in Europe and in North America. And, fossils of a fern, Glossopteris, which grew 250 million years ago, have been found in Australia and India.

Scientists found it remarkable that fossils of the same species were found thousands of miles apart, across great oceans. The only way these

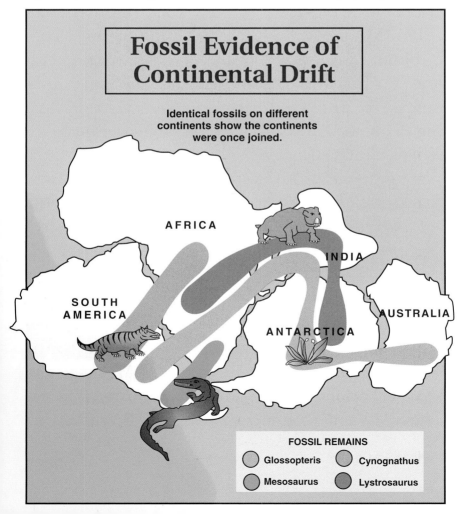

A museum display shows a stegosaurus skeleton. The animals migrated long distances when the continents were connected as one huge landmass.

plants and animals could have existed on different continents, they believe, is if the continents were once connected. Under these conditions, animals could have traveled freely from place to place. They could have spread seeds in their droppings or carried them on their fur or hides. Then, when the continents divided, animals and plants from one area were stuck in other areas. This explains how Stegosaurus could have lived on both the North American and Asian continents.

Using this and other evidence, scientists concluded that the continents had formed through movement of the tectonic plates. This movement had caused, and continues to cause, enormous changes in the earth. Mountains have formed, volcanoes have erupted, and **earthquakes** have shaken the land, all because of plate tectonics.

Chapter 2

How Mountains Form

The same forces that separated and moved the continents also created Earth's mountains. Shifting plates collide or move apart, causing rock and soil to pile up. Once these mounds of dirt and rock are more than two thousand feet higher than the surrounding terrain, they are called mountains. When this happens, one of three types of mountains is formed: folded, fault block, or volcanic.

Folded Mountains

When two continental plates collide, there is no place for the rock on the edges of the plates to go except up. The rock folds and piles up. The layers of rock are bent, but not broken. The folded layers show up as lines in the rock. Some angle sharply up from the ground. Others appear wavy. Folded mountains can be found throughout the world. In the United States, the Appalachian and Rocky Mountains are examples of folded mountains. The Alps in Switzerland and the Andes in South America also display the lines that indicate they were formed by folding.

The Himalayas are another example of folded mountains. They are a fifteen-hundred-mile-long range that runs along the border between Nepal and China. They formed 40 million to 60 million years ago, and they are the highest mountains in the world. These mountains began rising when the Indo-Australian plate pushed into the Asian plate. This process took millions of years. Little

The Rocky Mountains, which were formed by plate collision, stretch from Alaska through Canada and the continental United States to northern Mexico.

by little, one fold piled on top of another to create the world's highest peaks.

In the Himalayas is Mount Everest, the tallest mountain in the world. The rock on top of Mount Everest is marine limestone. This means the rock at 29,028 feet was once on the ocean floor. Scientists believe this happened when the plates collided and the surface of the earth folded. Rock from the ocean floor pushed upward as the land wrinkled and folded. The wrinkling and folding is a common feature of folded mountains.

The Indo-Australian plate is still moving into the Asian plate at the rate of about four inches a year. As the rock continues to fold, the Himalayas grow taller by about an inch a year.

The Himalayas formed when two plates collided into each other.

Scientists know this is happening because of a system they use called Global Positioning System, or GPS. GPS measures changes in the position of objects on Earth.

GPS bounces signals off satellites in orbit around Earth to objects being measured or located, then back again. Computers measure how long it takes for the signal to reach Earth and return to the orbiting satellite. By using GPS, scientists can determine exactly how much the Himalayas grow each year.

Fault Block Mountains

Sometimes, instead of plates pushing together, they pull apart. This type of movement forces layers of rock and soil to push up on either side of the **rift** or **fault**. When this happens, enormous chunks of rock break off, forming high, sharp peaks on either side of deep valleys.

The Aconcagua Mountains of Argentina, the Sierra Nevada mountain range of California and Nevada, and the Grand Tetons of Wyoming are all examples of fault block mountains. These mountains do not display wavy layers of rock like folded mountains. Instead, the rock in fault block mountains is sharp and craggy, as though building blocks had been heaped into a pile.

This is especially evident in the jagged Grand Teton Mountains. The Tetons are 40 miles long and 7 to 9 miles wide. These mountains were formed

The Grand Tetons in Wyoming are fault block mountains. Their sharp, jagged peaks tower high over deep valleys.

about 6 million to 9 million years ago around the Teton fault. Over millions of years, blocks of rock on either side of the fault moved. The west block rose to create the Tetons. The east block dropped to create the valley called Jackson Hole. The difference in elevation between the valley and the highest peaks is almost 30,000 feet.

The same type of rock can be found in the lowest parts of the valley and on the highest peaks of the mountains. This shows that the terrain was once all at the same level. Fault block mountains are among the most beautiful mountains

on Earth. The only mountains that are sometimes more spectacular are volcanic mountains.

Volcanic Mountains

Whenever a continental plate meets an oceanic
plate, a third type of mountain forms. This third
type is a volcanic mountain. Oceanic plates are
much heavier and denser than continental plates
because the weight of ocean water has com-
pressed them. When these plates meet, the
lighter continental plate rises, while the heavier
oceanic plate sinks beneath it. This process is
called **subduction**. The oceanic plate is sub-
ducted beneath the continental plate.

The oceanic plate pushes into the earth's crust
and may break into a layer of molten rock, called

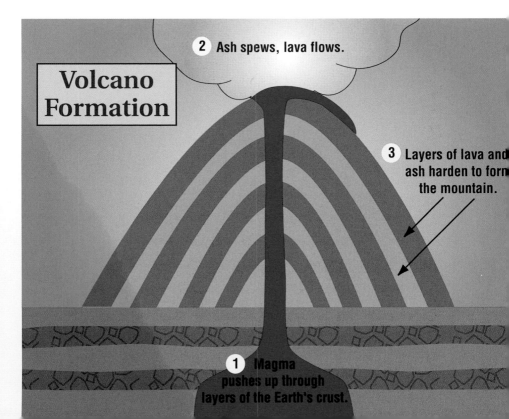

Volcano Formation

2 Ash spews, lava flows.

3 Layers of lava and ash harden to form the mountain.

1 Magma pushes up through layers of the Earth's crust.

magma. Tremendous heat produced by the magma escapes to the earth's surface, carrying magma with it. When magma reaches the surface, it is called **lava**. When lava piles up, cools, then hardens, a volcanic mountain is formed. It is usually shaped like a cone.

Volcanic mountains can form quickly—in a matter of days or weeks. This is because volcanic mountains are formed by tremendous heat and pressure. The heat and pressure cause rapid expansion of the ground before the **eruption**.

Examples of volcanic mountains include the Cascades in Washington, Oregon, and California; Popocatépetl in Mexico; and Mount Etna in northern Sicily. All of these mountains are shaped like cones. They do not display wavy layers like folded mountains, or sharp edges and corners like fault block mountains. Volcanic mountains often have a depression, or crater, in the top of the cone. This is where the top of the mountain was blown away when the volcano erupted.

Mount Etna

At eleven thousand feet, Mount Etna is Europe's highest active volcano. Mount Etna has been an active volcanic mountain for a long time. In the past fifty years, it has been especially active. Eruptions occur at the upper elevations of the mountain, producing slow-moving lava. These eruptions rarely kill people. People who live near

Steam pours from Europe's Mount Etna, in Sicily. Mount Etna is an active volcanic mountain that violently erupts from time to time.

the mountain know about its frequent eruptions and stay away.

The most recent eruption of Etna began on July 17, 2001. Heat from the earth's crust pushed against the surface, forming a huge cone that rose three hundred feet in one week. Mount Etna is one of the best examples of how quickly a volcanic mountain can form. When the lava cone exploded on July 21, the force rattled windows twenty miles away and hurled chunks of rock and lava as large as cars a mile into the sky. All mountains are majestic, but volcanic mountains are often the most spectacular.

Chapter 3

Mountains of Fire

Volcanoes are one of the most dramatic examples of the effects of plate tectonics. The word "volcano" comes from Vulcan, the Roman god of fire. A volcano is a place in the earth's crust that allows superheated molten rock to reach the earth's surface. This is called an eruption.

But not all volcanoes erupt. Active volcanoes are those that have erupted or shown signs of erupting within the past one hundred years. Volcanoes that have erupted within the past ten thousand years, but not in recent times, are called dormant volcanoes. If a volcano has not erupted in more than ten thousand years, and it is not expected to erupt ever again, it is considered extinct. Some extinct volcanoes, though, have erupted. Mount Vesuvius, in Italy, was believed to be extinct. However, it erupted in A.D. 79 and buried the towns of Pompeii and Herculaneum under a smothering blanket of ash, dust, and cinders.

Between nine hundred and thirteen hundred active volcanoes could erupt at any time. Most active volcanoes are located along the rim of the Pacific Ocean, where the Pacific plate meets several other plates. This ring of volcanoes is called the Ring of Fire. It goes from New Zealand north through Papua New Guinea, Indonesia, the Philippines, and Japan to the Kamchatka Peninsula of

An artist depicts what the eruption of Mount Vesuvius might have looked like.

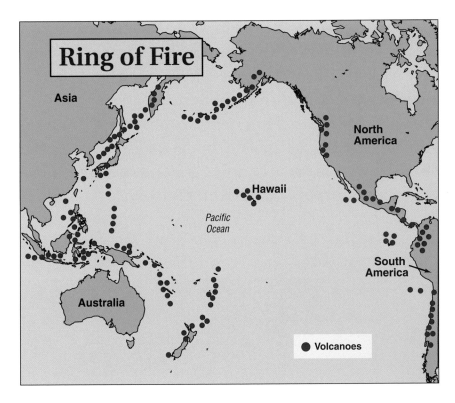

Ring of Fire

Asia

North America

Hawaii

Pacific Ocean

South America

Australia

● Volcanoes

eastern Russia. Then, the Ring of Fire runs east along the Aleutian Islands, and south along the western coastline of the United States.

In the Ring of Fire and elsewhere in the world, volcanoes are one of four types. Some erupt violently because of excessive heat and pressure causing them to explode. Others erupt less violently, when pressure is released more gradually. No matter how they erupt, volcanoes dramatically change the surface of the earth.

Shield Volcanoes

Shield volcanoes are the least explosive of all volcanoes. They occur when lava erupts through a **vent**, or an opening in the earth. The lava then spreads out, creating new rock on the earth's surface. This new rock is called **igneous rock**, which means rock from fire.

Shield volcanoes create low, broad, dome-shaped cones, or mountains. An example of a shield volcano is Mauna Loa in Hawaii. Mauna Loa consists of thousands of flows of lava, each less than fifty feet thick, piled on top of each other. Mauna Loa has erupted more than thirty times since 1843, and is the largest volcano in the world, covering half the island of Hawaii.

Kilauea, another shield volcano on the island of Hawaii, is the world's most active volcano. It

In this photo of Hawaii's Mauna Loa, taken from the space shuttle, dark lava flows can be seen on the volcano's slopes.

has been erupting continuously since January 3, 1983.

Cinder Cone Volcanoes

Cinder cone volcanoes are more violent than shield volcanoes. When cinder cone volcanoes erupt, fragments of rock, soil, and ash, called **tephra,** are thrown high in the air and fall back on the exploding mountain. One of the best known examples of a cinder cone volcano is Paricutin, in western Mexico. Before this volcano erupted in 1943, the ground was nothing more than a cornfield. No one had any idea there was a volcano there.

Within days of the eruption, a mountain was formed where the cornfield had been. It eventually rose to more than 1,350 feet. This volcano erupted for nine years, until 1952. The eruptions were violent in the beginning. Gradually, the number of eruptions declined. For the last six months of its eruptions, there were more violent explosions. Then, the volcano grew quiet at last. In nine years, the volcano produced twenty-three lava flows that destroyed two nearby towns.

Composite Volcanoes

The most violent eruptions come from composite volcanoes, also called strato volcanoes. Composite volcanoes have a central vent that spews both lava and tephra. The erupted material falls back on the mountain, creating a huge cone.

Ash and other volcanic debris spew from the mouth of this volcano.

Composite volcanoes erupt because of a build-up of gases inside the earth. Tremendous heat causes multiple explosions that produce huge clouds of hot ash and dust. The explosions blow most of the mountain away.

Mount Saint Helens, in Washington state in the United States, erupted on May 18, 1980. It is an example of the most violent type of eruption of a composite volcano. For two months before Mount Saint Helens exploded, scientists noted signs that the eruption was coming. One side of the mountain bulged because of pressure building inside. Steam and ash spewed from vents on the side of the mountain. The temperature of the rock on the mountain rose steadily. Eventually, violent explosions blew away the top and one side of the mountain.

Hot Spots

Most volcanoes are found along the edges of tectonic plates, where they collide. But some volcanoes occur in the center of plates. These are called hot spots. Enormous heat from volcanic activity deep inside the earth melts a hole in the center of the plate. Sometimes, magma reaches the surface. At other times, the heat of the hot spot produces boiling water or steam.

Beneath Yellowstone National Park is an active volcano caused by a hot spot. The heat from magma, deep inside the earth, heats underground water to the boiling point. The water then bubbles or gushes to the surface. Old Faithful, a geyser, shoots thousands of gallons of boiling water into the air about every seventy-six minutes. Old Faithful is only one of more than three hundred geysers in the park, all caused by the hot spot.

Mount Saint Helens fills the sky over Washington state with clouds of hot ash and dust.

The Hawaiian Islands were also created by a hot spot. An erupting volcano punched through the Pacific plate, creating a shield volcano. Lava piled up until an island was formed. As the plate moved slowly, another island was formed, then another and another.

Over millions of years, the hot spot created the Hawaiian Islands in the center of the Pacific plate. This hot spot is thought to be currently beneath the big island of Hawaii, which has several active volcanoes, including Kilauea and Mauna Loa.

No matter which type of eruption is about to occur, there are signs an eruption is coming. A vulcanologist—a scientist who studies volcanoes —can measure these signs and try to predict when the volcano will erupt.

Predicting Eruptions

Centuries ago, scientists had no way of knowing when a volcano was about to erupt. But as scientific knowledge grew and technology improved, they noticed patterns of events that happen just before an eruption. Gradually, they were able to make more precise predictions about when volcanoes were most likely to erupt.

Before a volcano erupts, the ground begins to expand from heat and pressure building in the earth's crust. The temperature of the rock and soil rises. Sometimes there are small earthquakes, which increase in intensity and frequency as the eruption gets closer.

Several instruments are used to predict volcanic eruptions. Tiltmeters and GPS systems measure the expansion of the ground in the area where the volcano is likely to occur. Seismometers detect earthquakes deep in the crust that, most of the time, are too small to be felt on the surface. Thermometers measure rises in temperature. Gas detectors measure increased amounts of gases, such as carbon dioxide and sulfur, that escape from within the earth prior to an eruption.

Predicting volcanic eruptions is still not an exact science. Using all the information gath-

A scientist examines lava in an effort to predict volcanic eruptions.

ered by measuring devices, vulcanologists can only guess when eruptions are going to occur. The most urgent of these indicators is the presence of earthquakes triggered by abrupt movements of tectonic plates deep within the earth.

Chapter 4

When the
Earth Shakes

An earthquake is a sudden movement of tectonic plates that causes the ground to shake. This occurs when pressure built up by the movement of tectonic plates causes the earth's crust to move or shift without warning. There are several ways this can happen. Tectonic plates may move side by side, going in the same direction but at different speeds. Or, they may move side by side, going in different directions. Sometimes, the plates press against each other and get stuck. That is when the largest quakes occur.

When the plates collide but cannot move past each other, tremendous pressure builds up between them. The result is much like what would happen if a car drove slowly into a wall. The car would stop when it reached the wall. If the accelerator were pressed, trying to make the car move forward, eventually the car would crumple or the wall would cave in. This is similar to what

Water flows where part of a road stretched before an earthquake tore it apart.

happens when tectonic plates, under tremendous pressure, suddenly give way.

When sections of the earth's crust jump past, move over, or slide under each other, the ground shakes, sometimes violently. Depending on where the movement occurs, vibrations sent through solid rock to the surface can be slight or can be destructive. These vibrations are called seismic waves. These waves can cause bridges to collapse and buildings to fall, depending on how deep within the earth the quake occurs.

Where Quakes Occur Inside the Earth

The deepest earthquake ever recorded occurred at 447 miles below the surface of the earth. Deep quakes do not cause as much damage to buildings and structures because seismic waves have to travel farther to reach them. The farther the waves have to travel, the less force they have when they reach the structures.

Shallow quakes cause the most damage to buildings and other structures because the waves do not have as far to travel through the earth. The earthquake that occurred in Kōbe, Japan, on January 17, 1995, was a shallow quake. The ground shook for about 20 seconds. The quake damaged or destroyed 180,000 buildings and killed 5,500 people. The amount of damage that occurs during

A man walks his bike past a leaning building that was destroyed during the Kōbe earthquake in 1995.

an earthquake depends on how much pressure has built up between the tectonic plates.

How Much Pressure Builds Between Plates?

The amount of pressure that builds between tectonic plates is hard to imagine. Pressure on rock can actually cause it to bend. This pressure stores energy in the rock. The same kind of energy is stored in a walnut when it is cracked. The more pressure exerted on the walnut, the more energy it contains. When it cannot store any more energy, the walnut breaks.

When too much pressure causes rock to break, all the energy stored in the rock is released in an instant. This can be as much as the energy of exploding 1 billion tons of dynamite. It is easy to see why buildings are shaken apart and bridges and houses collapse during an earthquake. It is as if a bomb had exploded under the ground.

Measuring Earthquakes

When an earthquake strikes, there are ways to measure its force. The best known measuring tool is the Richter scale. Earthquakes that measure more than 8.0 on the scale are considered great quakes. Only two of these have been recorded. The first occurred in Chile in 1960. This quake measured 9.5. The other took place in Alaska in 1964. That quake measured 9.2. Both earthquakes were truly catastrophic. They destroyed virtually every structure within miles of where the earthquakes occurred. They also caused tidal waves, fires, and explosions. Shock waves from the quake caused damage thousands of miles away in Hawaii, in Japan, in the Philippines, and on the West Coast of the United

States. Major quakes are those that measure 7.0 to 7.9. The 1995 Kōbe earthquake in Japan is considered a major quake because it measured 7.2 on the Richter scale.

Strong quakes, measuring 6.0 to 6.9 on the Richter scale, can also do a great deal of damage. On January 17, 1994, a strong quake struck North-ridge, California. The quake measured 6.7 on the

Earthquake survivors walk past a crane that is removing rubble from a destroyed building.

scale. It collapsed buildings and freeway inter-changes, and ruptured gas lines that caused fires.

Smaller earthquakes occur all the time. Most of these measure 1.0 to 3.0 and cannot be felt by people. They can be detected only with sensitive instruments. Scientists use these instruments to try and predict when earthquakes are about to happen.

Scientists use laser beams to detect slight movements in the earth. By examining these movements, scientists hope to be able to predict earthquakes.

Can Earthquakes Be Predicted?

Scientists could potentially save thousands of lives if they could predict when powerful earthquakes were going to happen. Predicting earthquakes is extremely difficult because no one knows when the energy stored in the rock will reach the point where it will be released in the form of a quake. There are signs, though, that can be noted and measured to help scientists guess when earthquakes are going to happen.

These signs include minor quakes, and the occasional shifting of rock along the fault. Scientists have instruments that measure expansion or movement of rock. Seismometers are instruments that record movement of rock in the earth. These instruments measure minor quakes. But instruments cannot predict exactly when a quake will occur. When minor quakes get stronger and closer together, a bigger earthquake may be about to happen.

Do Animals Know?

Scientists and others have noticed that animals seem to sense a quake's approach. People around the world have observed animals behaving differently just before an earthquake. Because of their acute senses, animals feel vibrations and changes in the earth that humans cannot detect. Pigs try to climb the walls of their pens before a

A dog gets checked for injuries after helping his owner survive being trapped under earthquake debris.

Plate Tectonics

quake, and chickens refuse to go inside their coops. Dogs run around frantically, sniffing and howling.

In the winter of 1974–1975, people in northeast China reported their animals behaving oddly. A series of small tremors had increased in strength and number over several months. Finally, an earthquake measuring 7.3 on the Richter scale struck the area on February 4, 1975. No one knows for certain if animal behavior can signal a coming earthquake.

Still Learning

Scientists still have a lot to learn. The more they learn about the movement of tectonic plates, the greater their chances of predicting when volcanoes will erupt and when earthquakes will shake the earth.

Glossary

continental drift: A theory that the continents moved across the earth's surface.

crust: The outermost shell of the earth.

earthquake: The vibration caused by seismic waves traveling outward from a sudden break or rupture in rocks beneath the surface.

eruption: When ash, lava flows, and gas are ejected from deep within the earth.

fault: A fracture in the earth's crust where movement has taken place.

igneous rock: Rock that is formed when magma cools and hardens.

lava: What magma is called when it reaches the surface of the earth.

magma: Molten rock when it is underground.

Pangaea: A supercontinent that existed 250 million years ago. It included most of the earth's continental landmasses.

plates: Segments of crust that the continents and oceans rest upon.

plate tectonics: The theory that the earth's outer shell is made up of separate pieces, or plates, which move and carry continents with them.

rift: A trough or valley formed where two blocks of crust move apart.

subduction: When one plate moves beneath another.

tephra: Rock fragments of all sizes thrown into the air above a volcano.

vent: An opening in the earth's surface through which volcanic ash, lava flows, and gas are emitted.

Books

Lori Andres and Jose Maria Miralles, illus., *Volcanoes*. New York: McClanahan Books, 1999. A big book packed with information, puzzles, and games. Readers explore how a volcano forms, what happens during an eruption, and how scientists measure its force.

Eric Arnold and Doug Knutson, illus., *Volcanoes: Mountains of Fire*. New York: Econo-Clad Books, 1999. The story of what makes volcanoes tick, along with accounts of some famous volcanic eruptions in history.

Melvin Berger, *As Old as the Hills*. Danbury, CT: Franklin Watts, 1989. This book explains how hills and mountains are formed, and the effects of erosion.

Franklyn Mansfield Branley and Richard Rosenblum, illus., *Earthquakes*. New York: Econo-Clad Books, 1999. Impressive photos, maps, drawings, and easy-to-read text about the effect of tectonic plate movement on man-made structures. Also includes advice on what to do if you are in an earthquake.

Nancy Field and Nancy Lynch, illus., *Discovering Earthquakes*. Middleton, WI: Dog-Eared Publications, 1995. A well-illustrated combination textbook and activity book. On one page, readers have to crack a secret code to discover the names of tectonic plates.

Bill Haduch, *Earthquake!* New York: Penguin U.S.A., 1999. An entertaining and informative book using humor and up-to-date facts. To illustrate earthquakes, readers pull a string and the whole book shakes!

Christopher F. Lampton, *Volcano.* Brookfield, CT: Millbrook Press, 1994. Color photos, diagrams, and maps. A well-written and helpful account of the development of a volcano, what causes eruptions, and how lava enriches the soil. Also illustrates the four types of volcanoes.

Cynthia Pratt Nicholson, *Earthquake!* Kids Can Press, 2002. Amazing photos and hands-on activities investigate the movement of tectonic plates and seismic waves. Also contains true-life stories of survival.

Helen Roney Sattler and Giulio Maestro, illus., *Our Patchwork Planet: The Story of Plate Tectonics.* New York: Lothrop, Lee & Shepard, 1995. This book uses satellite photos enhanced by computer technology and other color illustrations. Compares tectonic plates to vanilla wafers floating in chocolate pudding.

Fiona Watt, Jeremy Gower, and Chris Shields, *Earthquakes and Volcanoes.* London: Usborne/

EDC Publications, 1994. Numerous facts about earthquakes and volcanoes, with lively illustrations.

Websites

Geology—Plate Tectonics (www.ucmp.berkeley. edu). Excellent animation of how the continents were joined (Pangaea), and how they gradually moved apart until they reached the positions they hold today.

Plate Tectonics (www.outwood.wakefld. sch.uk). Information about continental drift, plate margins, and the San Francisco earthquake of 1989.

The ABC's of Plate Tectonics—Introduction (www.webspinners.com). An excellent site for beginners, with information about all the basics of plate tectonics, continental drift, and how mountains, volcanoes, and earthquakes result from the movement of tectonic plates.

A Science Odyssey—You Try It—Plate Tectonics (www.pbs.org). This site has an activity with a boiled egg, and information about the basics of plate tectonics, seafloor spreading, and continental drift. There are also profiles of several scientists, including Wegener and his original theory of continental drift.

Index

Aconcagua Mountains
(Argentina), 17
Africa, 10, 11
African plate, 6
Alaska, 36
Aleutian Islands, 24
Alps, 15
Andes, 15
Antarctica, 9, 11
Antarctic plate, 6
Appalachian Mountains, 14–15
Arabian plate, 6
Argentina, 17
Asian plate, 15–16
Atlantic Ocean, 9
Australia, 11

California, 17
carbon dioxide gas, 31
Caribbean plate, 6
Cascades, 20
chickens, 41
Chile, 36
China
animal reaction to earth-
quakes in, 41
folded mountains in, 15
Cocos plate, 6
continental drift theory
fossil evidence of, 10–13
continental plates, 4
crust, 4

Diadectid (insect), 11
dogs, 40–41
dynamite, 36

earth, 4
earthquakes, 13
animals and, 39–41
catastrophic, 6
deep, 34
major, 7
measuring, 36–38
plate collisions and, 32–34

prediction of, 39
pressure and 35–36
shallow quakes, 34
small, 38–39
strong, 37–38
Eurasian plate, 6
Europe, 11

fault, 17, 39

gas detectors, 31
Global Positioning System (GPS),
17, 30
Glossopteris (fern), 11
Grand Tetons (Wyoming), 17

Hawaiian Islands
Alaskan earthquake and, 36
creation of, 29
Herculaneum, Italy, 22
Himalayas, 15–17

Iceland, 9
India, 11
Indo-Australian plate, 6
Himalayas and, 15–17
Indonesia, 23
instruments, 9, 30–31

Jackson Hole, Wyoming, 18
Japan, 23
Juan de Fuca plate, 6

Kamchatka Peninsula (Russia),
23–24
Kilauea (Hawaii), 25–26,
30
Kōbe, Japan, 34, 37

laser beams, 38
lava, 20, 26
Lystrosaurus (reptile), 11

magma, 20
marine limestone, 16

Mauna Loa (Hawaii), 30
    as shield volcano, 24
Mesosaurus (reptile), 10
Mexico, 20
Mid-Atlantic Ridge, 10
mountains
    continental drift theory and, 8, 13
    fault block mountains, 17–19
    folded, 14–16
    volcanic, 19–21
Mount Etna (Sicily), 20–21
Mount Everest, 16
Mount Saint Helens (Washington), 27–28
Mount Vesuvius (Italy), 22

Nazca plate, 6
Nepal, 15
Nevada, 17
New Zealand, 23
North America, 11
North American plate, 6
Northridge, California, 37–38

ocean floor
    mapping of, 8–10
    mountains and valleys on, 9
oceanic plates, 4–5
Old Faithful (geyser), 28
Oregon, 20

Pacific Ocean, 23
Pangaea (supercontinent), 8
Papua, New Guinea, 23
Paricutin (Mexico), 26
Philippine plate, 6
Philippines
    Alaskan earthquake and, 36
    Ring of Fire and, 23
pigs, 39
plates, 4
    movement of, 6–7
    pressure and, 35–36
plate tectonics, 4, 13, 22
Pompeii, Italy, 22
Popocatépetl (Mexico), 20

radar, 9
Richter scale, 36
rift, 17

Ring of Fire, 23
Rocky Mountains, 15

Scotia plate, 6
seismometers, 30
Sicily, 20
Sierra Nevada, 17
sonar, 9
South America
    continental drift and, 10
    folded mountains in, 15
South American plate, 6
Stegosaurus (reptile), 11–13
subduction, 19
sulfur gas, 31
supercontinent, 7–8
Switzerland, 15

tephra, 26
Teton fault, 18
Texas, 11
thermometers, 31
tidal waves, 36
tiltmeters, 30

United States
    Alaskan earthquake and, 36–37
    folded mountains in, 14–15
    western coast of, 24

volcanoes, 13
    cinder cone volcano, 26
    composite volcano, 26–28
    eruption, 20
    hot spots, 29–30
    igneous rock, 24
    magma, 20
    molten rock, 4
    predicting, 30–31
    shield volcanoes, 24–26
    types of, 22–24
    vent, 24
Vulcan (Roman god of fire), 22

Washington, 20, 28
Wegener, Alfred Lothan, 7–8
Wyoming, 17–18

Yellowstone National Park (Wyoming), 29